Shabbat Anthology

Volume One

CD included

Editors

J. Mark Dunn & Joel N. Eglash

Project Manager & Typesetter

Eric S. Komar

Consulting Editor

Cantor Josée Wolff

Transcontinental Music Publications

More resources for Shabbat may be found at

www.TranscontinentalMusic.com and www.UAHCPress.com

The *Shabbat Anthology Volume I* CD accompanying this book is also available separately (TMP item no. 950106)

Track information on accompanying CD

1. L'chu N'ran'nah (Sirotkin) *•
featuring Cantor Jacob Mendelson
2. V'sham'ru
Danny Maseng
3. Niggun "Lubavitcher" •
featuring Cantor Bruce Ruben
4. Adon Olam (Aloni) *
featuring Cantor Bruce Ruben
5. Yism'chu (Solomon)
Safam
6. Mah Tovu
Danny Maseng
7. Lo Yisa Goi
Eric Komar
8. Mi-Chamochah (Lipson) *•
featuring Cantor Bruce Ruben
9. Adon Olam (Isle of Djerba) *
featuring Cantor Jill Abramson
10. Ki Eilecha
Shirona
11. Niggun "Y'did Nefesh" *
featuring Cantor Alane Katzew
12. Al Sh'loshah D'varim (Steinberg) *
featuring Cantor Josée Wolff
13. Shalom Rav
Steve Dropkin
14. Yih'yu L'ratzon / Oseh Shalom
Bonia Shur
15. Ahavat Olam (Mandell) *
featuring Cantor Josée Wolff
16. Niggun
featuring Cantor Jacob Mendelson
17. Sim Shalom (Isaacson)
featuring Cantor Thom King
18. Oseh Shalom (Steinberg) *
featuring Cantor Alane Katzew
19. Elohai N'tzor
Danny Maseng
20. Adonai Li
Cantor Bruce Benson
21. Shalom Rav (Eddleman) *
featuring Cantor Bruce Ruben
22. Mi-Chamochah
Cantor Richard Silverman
23. Niggun "Bialik" *•
featuring Cantor Josée Wolff
24. Adon Olam (Traditional)
Bonia Shur
25. Al Sh'loshah D'varim
Steve Dropkin
26. Niggun (Kazansky) *
featuring Cantor Jacob Mendelson
27. V'sham'ru (Finkelstein) *•
featuring Cantor Alane Katzew
28. Niggun "Kvell" (Eglash) *•
featuring Cantors Alane Katzew, Bruce Ruben, Kari Siegel-Eglash & Josée Wolff

* J. Mark Dunn: piano, bass recorder
• Joel N. Eglash: guitars, bass guitar

Hebrew Pronunciation Guide

VOWELS

a as in *father*
ai as in *aisle* (= long *i* as in *ice*)
e = short *e* as in *bed*
ei as in *eight* (= long *a* as in *ace*)
i as in *pizza* (= long *e* as in *be*)
o = long *o* as in *go*
u = long *u* as in *lunar*
ʻ = unstressed vowel close to ə or unstressed short *e*
oi as in *boy*

CONSONANTS

ch as in German *Bach* or Scottish *loch* (not as in *cheese*)
g = hard *g* as in *get* (not soft *g* as in *gem*)
tz = as in *boats*
h after a vowel is silent

SHABBAT ANTHOLOGY VOLUME ONE

A division of the Union of American Hebrew Congregations
633 Third Avenue - New York, NY 10017 - Fax 212.650.4109
212.650.4101 - www.TranscontinentalMusic.com - tmp@uahc.org

Manufactured in the United States of America
Cover design by Jackie Olenick
Book design by Joel N. Eglash
CD produced by J. Mark Dunn and Joel N. Eglash
ISBN 8074-0877-8
10 9 8 7 6 5 4 3 2 1

Preface

THIS IS THE FIRST in what will be an ongoing series of music for Shabbat. As composers and songwriters rise to meet the ever-growing demand for congregational service music, the *Shabbat Anthology* will serve as the vehicle for disseminating the best and most current of these, essentially making it a perpetually updating supplement to *Gates of Song*. In addition, the *Shabbat Anthology* will be a means of supplying fresh music to support all the of the Reform Jewish movement's prayer books.

BESIDES NEWLY WRITTEN music, the *Shabbat Anthology* also makes available excellent music that existed previously only in older through-composed services or in eighteenth generation photocopies of illegible manuscript. All pieces - with the exception of the *niggunim* (wordless melodies) - are provided with both a written-out keyboard accompaniment and chords for guitar. Another feature of this series is that it also contains arrangements of several pieces that began life as choral works. So often, cantors, soloists, and accompanists are faced with the challenge of arranging a choral piece (with a great melody) for solo or congregational singing. This book does that for you. Whenever possible, the composer was sought out to re-arrange his or her own music for this book. This is of great value for several reasons: Foremost, the composer has the opportunity to create a definitive solo arrangement of the piece; secondarily, it provides a model by which other pieces can be successfully adapted.

WE ARE THRILLED by this, the first installment of many in this series. The music is eclectic, well-written and arranged, and certain to become the 'traditional' of tomorrow; and though certain composers' works may be highlighted, the *Shabbat Anthology* will always be a broad-based and diverse resource. It remains for us to thank Cantors Josée Wolff and Alane Katzew for their invaluable assistance with music selection; Kenneth Gesser, publisher of the UAHC Press and Transcontinental Music; and especially Eric Komar, upon whose shoulders fell the Herculean task of typesetting and managing this project. Finally, we must thank all the composers and songwriters who provided the music for this volume. May the Divine prosper the work of our hands and voices.

J. Mark Dunn   Joel N. Eglash
7th May 2003
Yom Ha-atzmaut, 5763

table of contents

Mah Tovu
5 Danny Maseng - CD #6

L'chu N'ran'nah
10 R. Sirotkin, arr. Joyce Rosenzweig - CD #1

Ki Eilecha
13 Shirona - CD #10

Ahavat Olam
17 Eric Mandell - CD #15

Mi-Chamochah
20 Mark Lipson - CD #8
→ 22 Richard Silverman - CD #22

V'sham'ru
22 Meir Finkelstein, ed. Aryell Cohen - CD #27
28 Danny Maseng - CD #2

Yism'chu
31 Robbie Solomon - CD #5

Shalom Rav
36 Steve Dropkin, arr. Stephen Richards - CD #13
42 David Eddleman - CD #21

Sim Shalom
46 Michael Isaacson - CD #17

Elohai N'tzor
51 Danny Maseng - CD #19

Yih'yu L'ratzon / Oseh Shalom
56 Bonia Shur - CD #14

Oseh Shalom
58 Ben Steinberg - CD #18

Lo Yisa Goi
60 Eric Komar / Jordan Franzel - CD #7

Al Sh'loshah D'varim
67 Steve Dropkin - CD #25
70 Ben Steinberg - CD #12

Adon Olam
72 Traditional, arr. Bonia Shur - CD #24
78 Isle of Djerba, arr. Ben Steinberg - CD #9
82 Aminadav Aloni, arr. Christopher Hardin - CD #4

Adonai Li
85 Bruce Benson / Donald Rossoff, arr. Andrea Jill Higgins - CD #20

Niggun
93 Anonymous - CD #16

Niggun
93 Lubavitcher - CD #3

Niggun Bialik
94 Anonymous - CD #23

Niggun Y'did Nefesh
95 Anonymous - CD #11

Niggun
96 Boris Kazansky - CD #26

Niggun Kvell
96 Joel N. Eglash - CD #28

Shabbat Anthology Volume I

Shabbat Anthology Volume I

Mah Tovu

מה טבו

CD track 6

***Music:** Danny Maseng, arr. J. Mark Dunn*
***Text:** Numbers 24:5; Psalms 5:8, 26:8, 95:6, & 69:14*

13
Am7 Am7/C D G G/F♯ Em Em7/D
mah to - - - vu o - ha - le - cha Ya - a - kov
17
C Am7 D7sus4 D G V1&2 Em Em/D
mish - k' - no - te - cha Yis - - - ra - - - eil. 1. Va - a - ni b' - rov chas - d' -
2. A - do - nai a - hav - - -
21
C Em/B Am Am/G D/F♯ D E♭ F
cha a - vo vei - te - - - cha, esh - ta - cha - veh hei -
ti m' - on bei - te - - - cha, um' - kom mish - kan k' - vo -
25
B♭ Gm7/D Gm Cm A7 1. D 2. V3
chal kod - sh' - cha b' - yir - a - te - - - cha. 3. Va - a -
de - - - cha, mish - kan k'vo - de - - - - - - - - - - - - cha.

29
Em
Em/D
C
Em/B
Am
Am/G
D/F♯
D
ni esh - ta - cha - veh v' - ech - ra - ah, ev - r'-
33
E♭
F
Cm
A7
D
Esus4
E
cha lif - nei A - do - nai o - - - - - - si.
Ch2
37
A
E
F♯m
Bm7
Bm7/D
E
Mah to - - - vu, mah to - - - vu
41
A
A/G♯
F♯m
F♯m7/E
D
Bm7
E7sus4
E7
o - ha - le - cha Ya - a - kov mish - k' - no - te - cha Yis - ra - eil.

45
A E F♯m Bm7 Bm7/D E
Mah to - - - vu, mah to - - - vu
49
A A/G♯ F♯m F♯m7/E D Bm7/D E7sus4/D E7
to Coda
o - ha - le - cha Ya - a - kov mish-k'-no-te - cha Yis - - - ra - - -
to Coda
53
A Br F♯m7 Bm7 E7 A D E7
eil. Va - a - ni t'- fi - la - ti l'-cha, A - do - nai eit ra -
57
A C♯m7♭5 C♯♭9 F♯7 Bm Bm7/A G G♯°
tzon. E - lo - him, b'-rov chas - de - - - cha, E - lo - him, b'-rov chas -

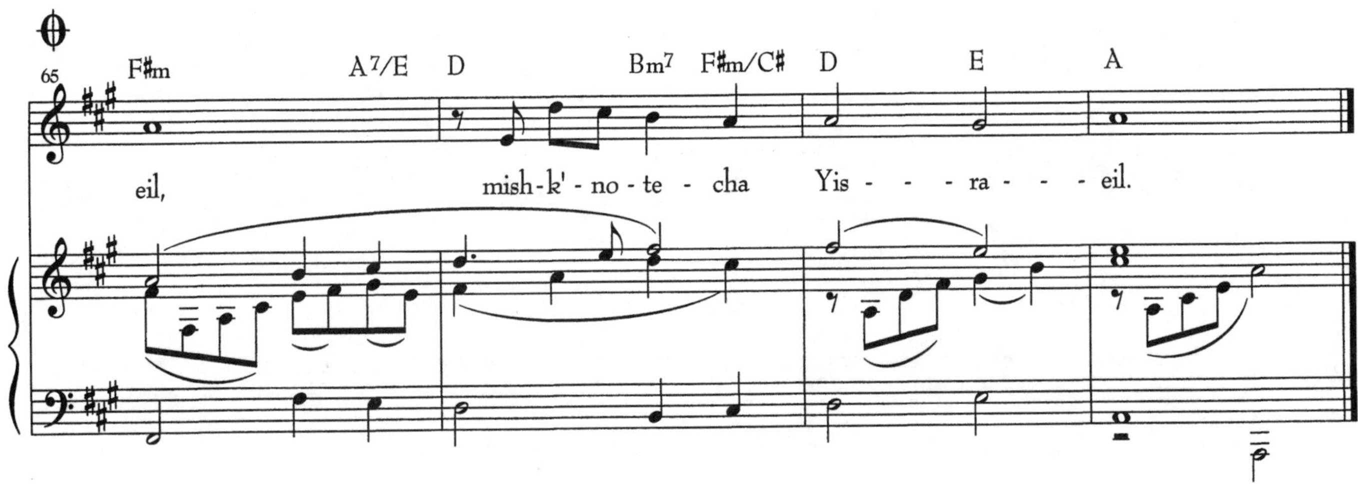

How lovely are your tents, O Jacob, your dwelling-places, O Israel! In Your abundant lovingkindness, God, let me enter Your house to worship reverently in Your holy temple. God, I love Your house, the place where Your glory dwells. So I would worship with humility, I would seek blessing in the presence of God, my Maker. To You, then, God, does my prayer go forth. May this be a time of joy and favor. In Your great love, O God, answer me with Your saving truth.

מַה־טֹּבוּ אֹהָלֶיךָ, יַעֲקֹב מִשְׁכְּנֹתֶיךָ, יִשְׂרָאֵל!
וַאֲנִי, בְּרֹב חַסְדְּךָ אָבוֹא בֵיתֶךָ,
אֶשְׁתַּחֲוֶה אֶל־הֵיכַל קָדְשְׁךָ בְּיִרְאָתֶךָ.
יְיָ אָהַבְתִּי מְעוֹן בֵּיתֶךָ וּמְקוֹם מִשְׁכַּן כְּבוֹדֶךָ
וַאֲנִי אֶשְׁתַּחֲוֶה וְאֶכְרָעָה אֶבְרְכָה לִפְנֵי־יְיָ עֹשִׂי
וַאֲנִי תְפִלָּתִי לְךָ, יְיָ, עֵת רָצוֹן.
אֱלֹהִים, בְּרָב־חַסְדֶּךָ עֲנֵנִי בֶּאֱמֶת יִשְׁעֶךָ.

L'chu N'ran'nah

לכו נרננה

Music: R. Sirotkin, arr. Joyce Rosenzweig
Text: Psalm 95:1-2

CD track (1)

10
Em B7 B Em
nai. Na - ri - a, na - ri - a l' - tzur yish - ei - nu n' - kad -
13
Am Am7/D G B7 Em
mah fa - nav b' - to - dah. Na - ri - a, na - ri - a l' -
16
Am B7 Em
tzur yish - ei - nu biz - mi - rot na - ri - a lo. L' - chu n' -
19
C Em Em/D Am/C Am D D/F#
ra - n' - nah, l' - chu n' - ra - n' - nah, l' - chu n' - ra - n' - nah la - do -

Go forth singing songs of joy to the Eternal. Let us shout to our Savior. Let us turn to God with thanks. Let us shout to our Savior with a joyous song.

לְכוּ נְרַנְּנָה לַיי.
נָרִיעָה לְצוּר יִשְׁעֵנוּ, נְקַדְּמָה פָנָיו בְּתוֹדָה.
נָרִיעָה לְצוּר יִשְׁעֵנוּ בִּזְמִרוֹת נָרִיעַ לוֹ.

Ki Eilecha

CD track (10)

Music: *Shirona*
Text: *Sabbath liturgy - An'im Z'mirot*

Gently, with expression ♩= 104

(gtr. capo 1)

Chords (mm. 1–5): D/E♭ – F♯m/Gm – D/E♭ E/F – F♯m/Gm – D/E♭ E/F

mp

Chords (mm. 6–11): A/B♭ F♯m/Gm – D/E♭ E/F – F♯m/Gm – V1&2 – Bm/Cm – D/E♭

1. An - im z'mi - rot v'-shi -
(2.) shi cham - dah b'-

mp

Chords (mm. 12–16): F♯m/Gm – C♯m/Dm – A/B♭ – Bm/Cm D/E♭ – D/E♭ E/F

rim e - e - rog Ki ei - le - cha naf - shi ta - - - a -
tzeil ya - de-cha la - da - at, la - da - at kol raz so - de -

17
F#m Gm
Ch
D E♭
F#m Gm
D E♭ E F
rog
cha.
Ki ei - le - cha, ki ei -
mf
22
F#m Gm
D E♭ E F A B♭ F#m Gm
D E♭ E F
1. F#m Gm
le - - cha, ki ei - le - cha naf - shi ta - a - rog.
27
2. F#m Gm
D E♭
F#m Gm
D E♭ E F
2.Naf - rog. Ki ei - le - cha, ki ei -
32
F#m Gm
D E♭ E F A B♭ F#m Gm
D E♭ E7 F7
E F
le - - cha, ki ei - le - cha naf - shi ta - a - rog

37 E/F — Br — Em/Fm — Em7/Fm7 — C/D♭ — B/C — C/D♭

_ Mi - dei dab - ri bich' - vo - de - - - - cha. Ho - meh li -

cresc.

43 G/A♭ — D/E♭ — G/A♭ — Am/B♭m — Bm/Cm — C♯m/Dm

bi el do - de - - - - cha. Ho - meh__ li - bi__ ho - meh__ li -

dim.

49 F♯/G — V3 — Bm/Cm — D/E♭ — F♯m/Gm — C♯m/Dm

bi.__ Al kein__ a - da - beir__ b' - cha nich - ba - dot__ V' - shim -

un poco rit.

55 A/B♭ — Bm/Cm — D/E♭ — D/E♭ — E/F — F♯m/Gm

cha a - cha - beid__ b' - shi - rei_ y' - di - dot__

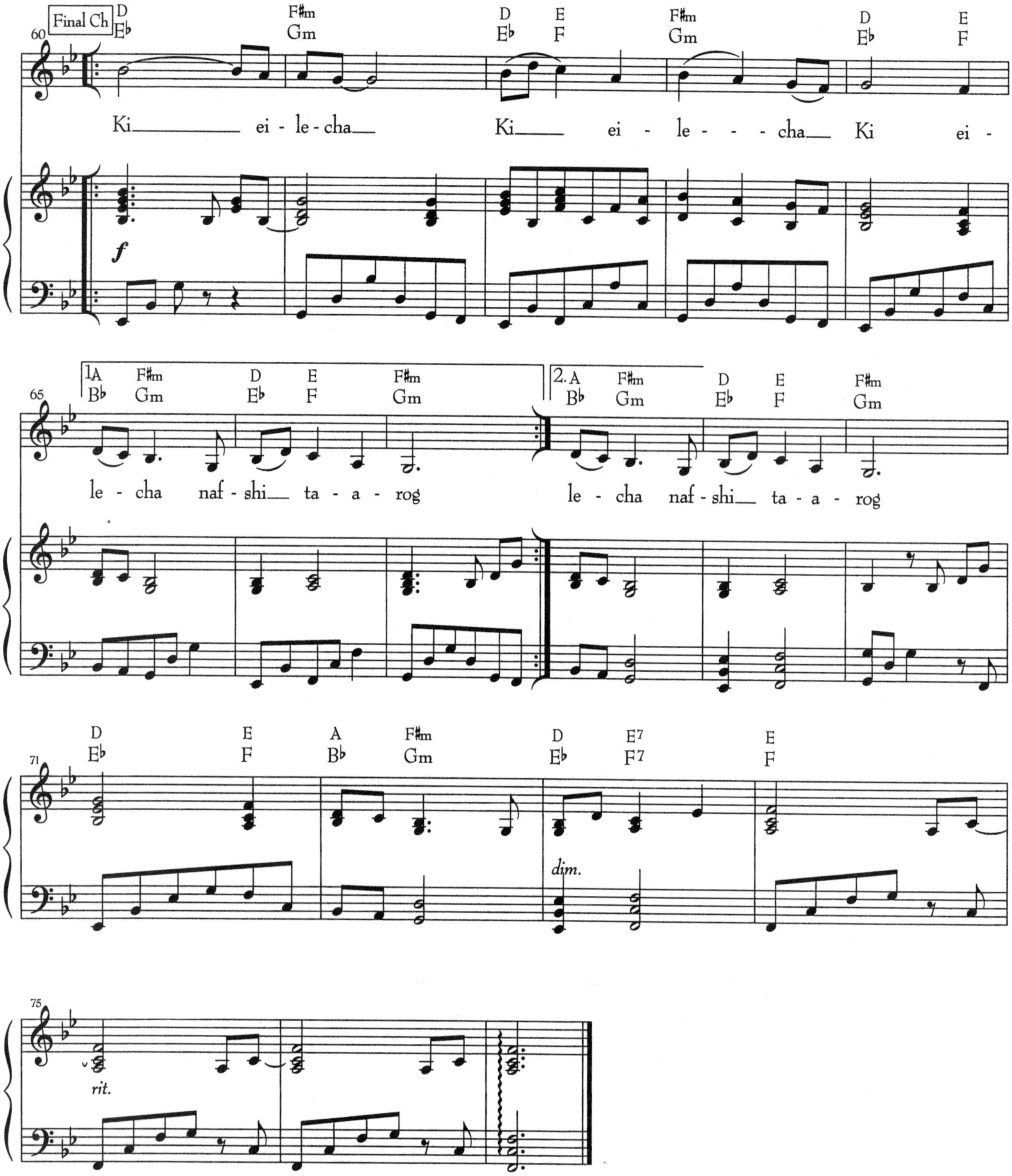

Final Ch

D E♭ | F♯m Gm | D E♭ E F | F♯m Gm | D E♭ E F

Ki___ ei - le - cha___ Ki___ ei - le - - - cha___ Ki ei -

f

1. A B♭ F♯m Gm | D E♭ E F | F♯m Gm || 2. A B♭ F♯m Gm | D E♭ E F | F♯m Gm

le - cha naf - shi___ ta - a - rog | le - cha naf - shi___ ta - a - rog

D E♭ | E F | A B♭ F♯m Gm | D E♭ E7 F7 | E F

dim.

I make pleasant songs, and weave verses, because my soul longs for You. To know Your deepest secret, to be in Your hand's shade, is my soul's strongest wish. My heart yearns for Your love, whenever I speak of Your glory. So may my thought be sweet to You, for whom my soul longs.

אַנְעִים זְמִירוֹת וְשִׁירִים אֶאֱרוֹג,
כִּי אֵלֶיךָ נַפְשִׁי תַעֲרוֹג.
נַפְשִׁי חָמְדָה בְּצֵל יָדֶךָ, לָדַעַת
כָּל־רָז סוֹדֶךָ. מִדֵּי דַבְּרִי בִּכְבוֹדֶךָ,
הוֹמֶה לִבִּי אֶל־דּוֹדֶיךָ. יֶעֱרַב־נָא
שִׂיחִי עָלֶיךָ, כִּי נַפְשִׁי תַעֲרוֹג אֵלֶיךָ.

Ahavat Olam

אהבת עולם

Music: Eric Mandell, arr. J. Mark Dunn
Text: Evening liturgy

CD track (15)

11
Em E7 Am D D7
kein, A - do - nai E - lo - hei - - - - nu, b'-shoch-bei - - - nu u - v' - ku -
14
G Em C Am7 Em B
mei - - - - nu na - si - ach, b'-chu-ke - - - - - cha v'-nis-
17
Em E7 Am D7
mach b' - div - rei To - ra - te - - - - cha u - - - v'-mitz - - - vo -
20
Em C Am7 Bm7 Em7 Em Am Em
te - - - cha l'-o-lam va - - - ed. Ki heim cha -

אַהֲבַת עוֹלָם בֵּית יִשְׂרָאֵל עַמְּךָ אָהָבְתָּ.
תּוֹרָה וּמִצְוֹת, חֻקִּים וּמִשְׁפָּטִים אוֹתָנוּ לִמַּדְתָּ.
עַל־כֵּן, יְיָ אֱלֹהֵינוּ, בְּשָׁכְבֵּנוּ וּבְקוּמֵנוּ נָשִׂיחַ בְּחֻקֶּיךָ,
וְנִשְׂמַח בְּדִבְרֵי תוֹרָתְךָ וּבְמִצְוֹתֶיךָ לְעוֹלָם וָעֶד.
כִּי הֵם חַיֵּינוּ וְאֹרֶךְ יָמֵינוּ וּבָהֶם נֶהְגֶּה יוֹמָם וָלָיְלָה.
וְאַהֲבָתְךָ אַל־תָּסִיר מִמֶּנּוּ לְעוֹלָמִים!
בָּרוּךְ אַתָּה, יְיָ, אוֹהֵב עַמּוֹ יִשְׂרָאֵל.

Unending is Your love for Your people, the House of Israel: Torah and Mitzvot, laws and precepts have You taught us. Therefore, Eternal God, when we lie down and when we rise up, we will meditate on Your laws and rejoice in Your Torah and Mitzvot for ever. Day and night we will reflect on them, for they are our life and the length of our days. Then Your love shall never depart from our hearts! We praise You, Eternal God, who loves our people Israel.

Mi-Chamochah

מי-כמכה

Music: Mark Lipson
Text: Exodus 15:11, 18; Jeremiah 31:10

CD track 8

Who is like You, Eternal One, among the gods that are worshiped? Who is like You, majestic in holiness, awesome in splendor, doing wonders?

In our escape from the sea, Your children saw You display Your power. "This is my God!" they cried.

We, the redeemed, sang a new song to Your name. At the shore of the Red Sea, saved from destruction, we proclaimed Your sovereign power: "The Eternal shall reign for ever and ever!" "The Eternal will reign for ever and ever!"

מִי־כָמֹכָה בָּאֵלִם, יְיָ? מִי כָּמֹכָה, נֶאְדָּר בַּקֹּדֶשׁ,
נוֹרָא תְהִלֹּת, עֹשֵׂה פֶלֶא?

מַלְכוּתְךָ רָאוּ בָנֶיךָ, בּוֹקֵעַ יָם לִפְנֵי
מֹשֶׁה; ״זֶה אֵלִי!״ עָנוּ וְאָמְרוּ:

שִׁירָה חֲדָשָׁה שִׁבְּחוּ גְאוּלִים לְשִׁמְךָ
עַל־שְׂפַת הַיָּם; יַחַד כֻּלָּם הוֹדוּ וְהִמְלִיכוּ
וְאָמְרוּ: ״יְיָ יִמְלֹךְ לְעוֹלָם וָעֶד!״

Mi-Chamochah

מי-כמכה

Music: Richard Silverman
Text: Exodus 15:11, 18; Jeremiah 31:10

CD track (22)

Who is like You, Eternal One, among the gods that are worshiped? Who is like You, majestic in holiness, awesome in splendor, doing wonders?

מִי־כָמֹכָה בָּאֵלִם, יְיָ? מִי כָּמֹכָה, נֶאְדָּר בַּקֹּדֶשׁ,
נוֹרָא תְהִלֹּת, עֹשֵׂה פֶלֶא?

In our escape from the sea, Your children saw You display Your power. "This is my God!" they cried. "The Eternal shall reign for ever and ever!"

מַלְכוּתְךָ רָאוּ בָנֶיךָ, בּוֹקֵעַ יָם לִפְנֵי
מֹשֶׁה; "זֶה אֵלִי!" עָנוּ וְאָמְרוּ:

We, the redeemed, sang a new song to Your name. At the shore of the Red Sea, saved from destruction, we proclaimed Your sovereign power: "The Eternal shall reign for ever and ever!"

שִׁירָה חֲדָשָׁה שִׁבְּחוּ גְאוּלִים לְשִׁמְךָ
עַל־שְׂפַת הַיָּם; יַחַד כֻּלָּם הוֹדוּ וְהִמְלִיכוּ
וְאָמְרוּ: "יְיָ יִמְלֹךְ לְעוֹלָם וָעֶד!"

V'sham'ru

ושמרו

Music: Meir Finkelstein, ed. Aryell Cohen
Text: Sabbath liturgy

CD track (27)

Originally published for unison choir, Cantor, congregation, and keyboard (991347).

11
Em Fm A/E B♭/F C/E D♭/F Em Fm Cmaj7 D♭maj7 D7 E♭7
sha - - m'-ru v' - nei Yis-ra - eil et ha-Sha - - - -
14
Gmaj7 A♭maj7 A B♭ B C Em Fm A/E B♭/F C/E D♭/F Em Fm
bat la - - - a-sot et ha-Sha - bat l' -
17
Am7 B♭m7 rit. Bm7 Cm7 Fine ♩= 72 Solo: V1 G A♭ Cm6/G D♭m6/A♭
do-ro-tam b'-rit o - - lam. Bei - ni u-vein b'-nei Yis-ra -
rit.
Fine
20
G A♭ Cm6/G D♭m6/A♭ G A♭ Cm6(add11)/G D♭m6(add11)/A♭ G A♭ Dm/F E♭m/G♭
eil, bei - ni u - vein b' - nei Yis - ra - eil
rit.

23
E E/G♯ Am D Gmaj7 B7/A C A7 Am/D D
F F/A B♭m E♭ A♭maj7 C7/B♭ D♭ B♭7 B♭m/E♭ E♭
ot hi l' - o - - - - lam, ot hi l' - o -
a tempo
Solo:
26
Gmaj7 A B G Cm6/G G Cm/G
A♭maj7 B♭ C A♭ D♭m6/A♭ A♭ D♭m/A♭
All: D.S.
V2
Freely
lam. V' - Ki shei - shet ya - - - mim,
D.S.
29
G Cm6(add11)/G G D/F E E/G♯ Am D
A♭ D♭m6(add11)/A♭ A♭ E♭/G♭ F F/A B♭m E♭
ki shei - shet ya - - - mim a - - - sah A -
rit.
a tempo
32
Gmaj7 B7/A C A7 Am/D D7 Gmaj7 A B
A♭maj7 C7/B♭ D♭ B♭7 B♭m/E♭ E♭7 A♭maj7 B♭ C
All: D.S.
do - - - nai et ha - sha - ma - yim v' - - et ha - - a - - - retz. V'
D.S.

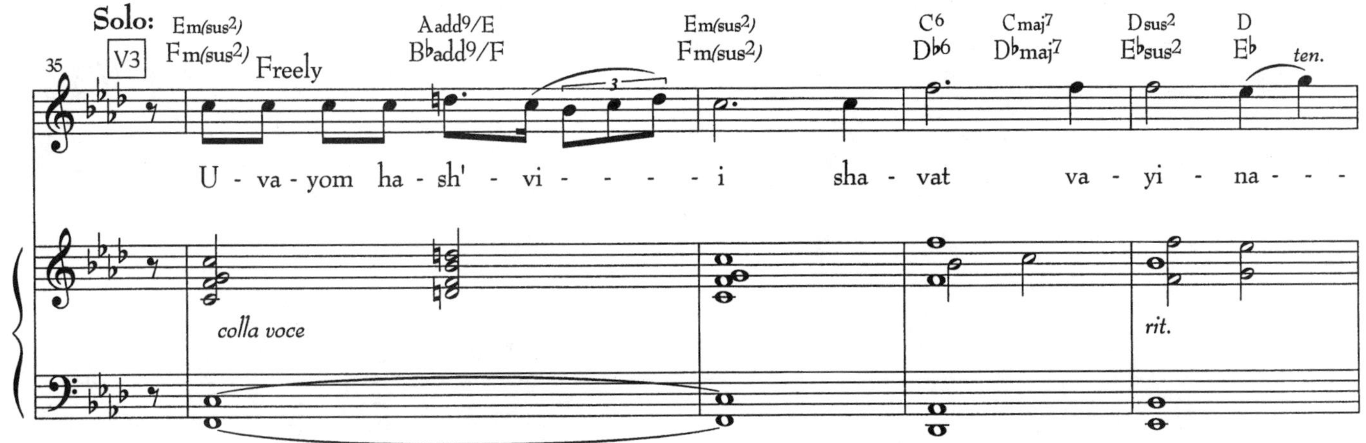

The people of Israel shall keep the Sabbath, observing the Sabbath in every generation as a covenant for all time. It is a sign between Me and the people of Israel. For in six days the Eternal God made heaven and earth, and on the seventh day God rested from labor and was refreshed.

וְשָׁמְרוּ בְנֵי־יִשְׂרָאֵל אֶת־הַשַּׁבָּת
לַעֲשׂוֹת אֶת־הַשַּׁבָּת לְדֹרֹתָם בְּרִית עוֹלָם.
בֵּינִי וּבֵין בְּנֵי יִשְׂרָאֵל אוֹת הִיא לְעֹלָם.
כִּי שֵׁשֶׁת יָמִים עָשָׂה יְיָ אֶת־הַשָּׁמַיִם וְאֶת־הָאָרֶץ,
וּבַיּוֹם הַשְּׁבִיעִי שָׁבַת וַיִּנָּפַשׁ.

V'sham'ru

ושמרו

Music: Danny Maseng, arr. J. Mark Dunn
Text: Sabbath liturgy

CD track (2)

12
F♯m D A E F♯m E
eil et ha - Sha - bat, et ha - Sha - bat la - a - sot et ha - Sha -
16
A F♯m Dm E to Coda 1. A V1 A E
bat l' - do - ro - tam b' - rit o - lam. Bei - ni u - vein b' -
to Coda
20
F♯m D Bm F♯m E A F♯m7 A7
nei Yis - ra - eil ot hi l' - o - lam, l' - o - lam. Bei - ni u - vein b' -
24
F♯ Bm D B7 E E7 2. A V2
nei Yis - ra - eil ot hi l' - o - lam, l' - o - lam. V' - sha - m' - lam. Ki

The people of Israel shall keep the Sabbath,
observing the Sabbath in every generation
as a covenant for all time. It is a sign between
Me and the people of Israel. For in six days
the Eternal God made heaven and earth,
and on the seventh day God rested from labor
and was refreshed.

וְשָׁמְרוּ בְנֵי־יִשְׂרָאֵל אֶת־הַשַּׁבָּת
לַעֲשׂוֹת אֶת־הַשַּׁבָּת לְדֹרֹתָם בְּרִית עוֹלָם.
בֵּינִי וּבֵין בְּנֵי יִשְׂרָאֵל אוֹת הִיא לְעֹלָם.
כִּי שֵׁשֶׁת יָמִים עָשָׂה יְיָ אֶת־הַשָּׁמַיִם וְאֶת־הָאָרֶץ,
וּבַיּוֹם הַשְּׁבִיעִי שָׁבַת וַיִּנָּפַשׁ.

Yism'chu

ישמחו

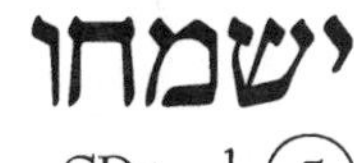

CD track (5)

Music: *Robbie Solomon*
Text: *Sabbath liturgy*

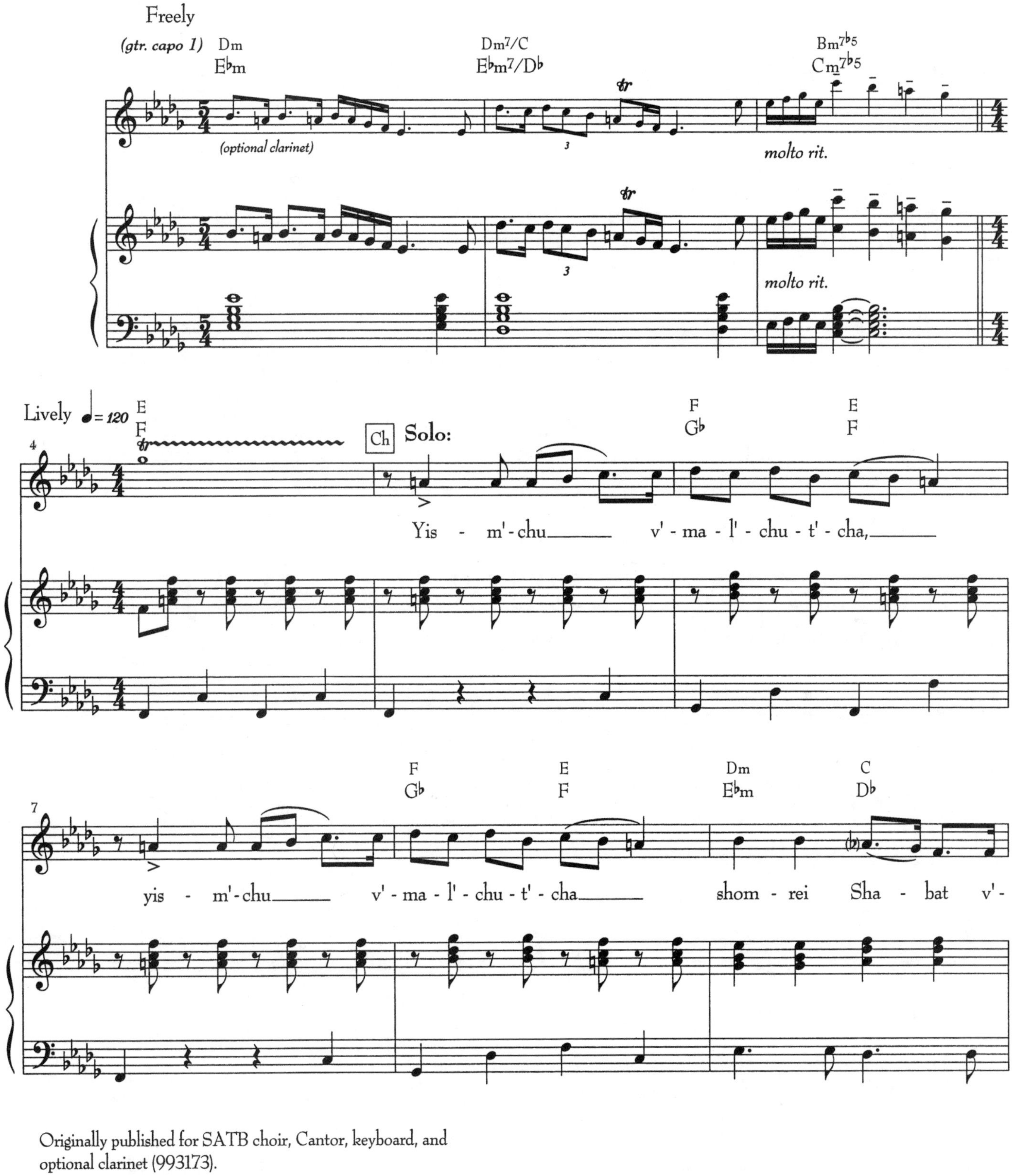
Freely
(gtr. capo 1)
Dm
E♭m
Dm7/C
E♭m7/D♭
Bm7♭5
Cm7♭5
(optional clarinet)
molto rit.
molto rit.
Lively ♩= 120
E
F
F
G♭
E
F
Ch
Solo:
Yis - m'-chu v' - ma - l' - chu - t' - cha,
F
G♭
E
F
Dm
E♭m
C
D♭
yis - m'-chu v' - ma - l' - chu - t' - cha shom - rei Sha - bat v'-

Originally published for SATB choir, Cantor, keyboard, and optional clarinet (993173).

B♭ Am Bm7♭5 E7 E
C♭ B♭m Cm7♭5 F7 F
All:
(small notes: optional harmony)
kor - ei o - neg, o - neg Sha - - - bat. Yis - m'-chu v'-
F E E F E
G♭ F F G♭ F
ma - l' - chu - t' - cha, yis - m'-chu v' - ma - l' - chu - t' - cha
Dm C B♭ Am Bm7♭5
E♭m D♭ C♭ B♭m Cm7♭5
shom - rei Sha - bat v' - kor - ei o - neg, o - neg Sha - - -
1., 2. E7 Am G
F7 B♭m A♭
Solo:
V
bat. 1. Am m' - ka - d' - shei sh' - vi - - - i, Am
2. V' - ha - - sh' - vi - - - i ra - tzi - ta bo ra -

Dm F C E7 Am
E♭m G♭ D♭ F7 B♭m
m' - ka - d' - shei sh' - vi - i, Sha - bat. Ku - - lam
tzi - ta bo v' - ki - dash - to, Sha - bat. Chem - - - dat ya -
G Dm F E7 Am
A♭ E♭m G♭ F7 B♭m
yis - b'- u v' - yit - an - gu mi - tu - ve - cha, Sha - bat.
mim o - to ka - ra - ta, ka - ra - ta, Sha - bat.
Solo - Recititive:
3. E7
F7
Br
Am
B♭m
bat. Zei - cher l' - ma - - - - - - - seih, l' -
colla voce
G F E7 Dm
A♭ G♭ F7 E♭m
ma - a - seih v' - rei - - - shit, zei - - - - - - - cher l' -

Bm7b5
Cm7b5
Tempo I
E
F
Final Ch
All:
ma - a - seih, l' - ma - a - seih v'- rei - - - - - - shit. Yis - m'- chu v'-
Tempo I
F
Gb
E
F
Yis - m' - chu
ma - l' - chu - t' - cha, yis - m'- chu v' - ma - l' - chu - t' - cha
Dm
Ebm
C
Db
Bb
Cb
Am
Bbm
Bm7b5
Cm7b5
shom - rei Sha - bat v' - kor - ei o - neg, o - neg Sha - bat. Yis - m'- chu v'-
ma - l' - chu - t' - cha, yis - m'- chu v' - ma - l' - chu - t' - cha

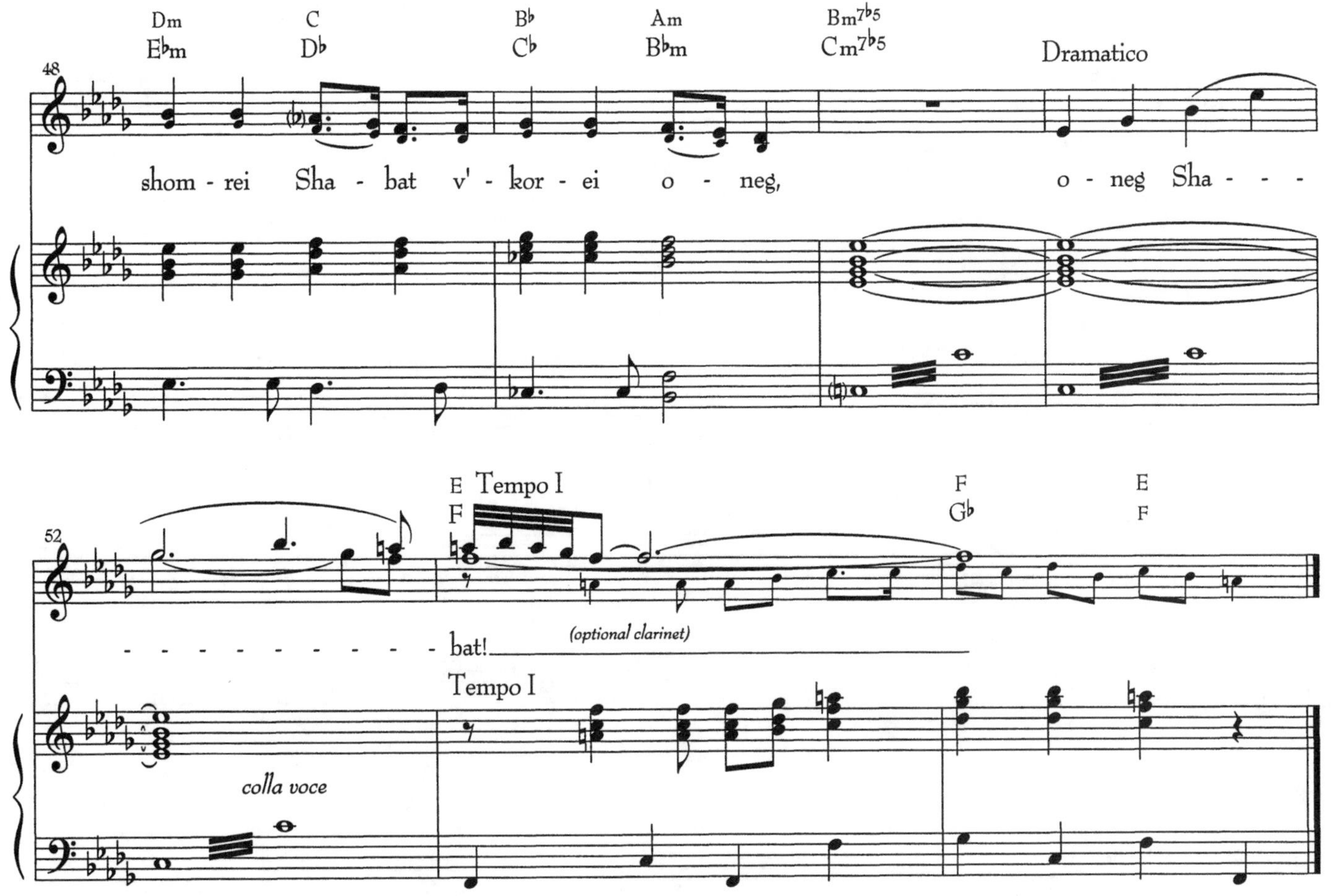

Those who keep the Sabbath and call it a delight shall rejoice in Your deliverance. All who make the seventh day holy shall be gladdened by Your goodness. This day is Israel's festival of the spirit, sanctified and blessed by You, the most precious of days, a symbol of the joy of creation.

יִשְׂמְחוּ בְמַלְכוּתְךָ שׁוֹמְרֵי שַׁבָּת וְקוֹרְאֵי עֹנֶג.
עַם מְקַדְּשֵׁי שְׁבִיעִי כֻּלָּם יִשְׂבְּעוּ
וְיִתְעַנְּגוּ מִטּוּבֶךָ. וְהַשְּׁבִיעִי רָצִיתָ
בּוֹ וְקִדַּשְׁתּוֹ. חֶמְדַּת יָמִים אוֹתוֹ קָרָאתָ,
זֵכֶר לְמַעֲשֵׂה בְרֵאשִׁית.

Shalom Rav

שלום רב

Music: Steve Dropkin, arr. Stephen Richards
Text: Liturgy

CD track (13)

Originally published for SATB choir, solo voice, and keyboard (993195).

13 All: Em A D G G/F#
Sha - - - lom rav al Yis - ra - eil am - cha ta -
17 Em Am Bsus4 B Em
Solo: mf
sim, ta - sim l' - o - lam. Ki A -
f
21 D D/C Em/B Em
tah Hu Me - lech A - don l' - -
mp
25 D/F# D7/F# Em Em/G A
chol ha - sha - lom. Ki A -

29
D
D/F♯
G
Em
tah Hu Me - lech A - don l' - -
mf
33
Am
A♯°
Badd9
B7
chol ha - sha - lom.
All:
37
Em
A
D
D7
G
G/B
p
Sha - - - lom rav al Yis - ra - eil am - cha ta -
p
41
C
C/G
C
Am
Am7
B7
sim, ta - sim l' - - o - - lam.

45
Em
A
D
D7
G
G/F#
Sha - - - lom rav al Yis - ra - eil am - cha ta -
49
Em
Am7
Bsus4
B
Em
Solo:
mf
sim, ta - sim l' - o - lam. V' -
53
F
Em
Dm7
Em
B7/E
Em
mf
tov b' - ei - ne - cha l' - va - reich
57
D
Em/D
D7
Em
f
et am - cha Yis - ra - eil b' -

61
F Em Dm7 Gmaj7 Gmaj7/F# Em Em/D
chol eit u - v' - chol sha - ah
65
Am/C Am/B A A7 Bsus4 B
bish - - lo - me - - - - cha.
All:
69
Em A D D7 G G/B
p
Sha - - lom rav al Yis - ra - eil am - cha ta -
p
73
C C/G C B/A B7
sim, ta - sim l' - o - lam.

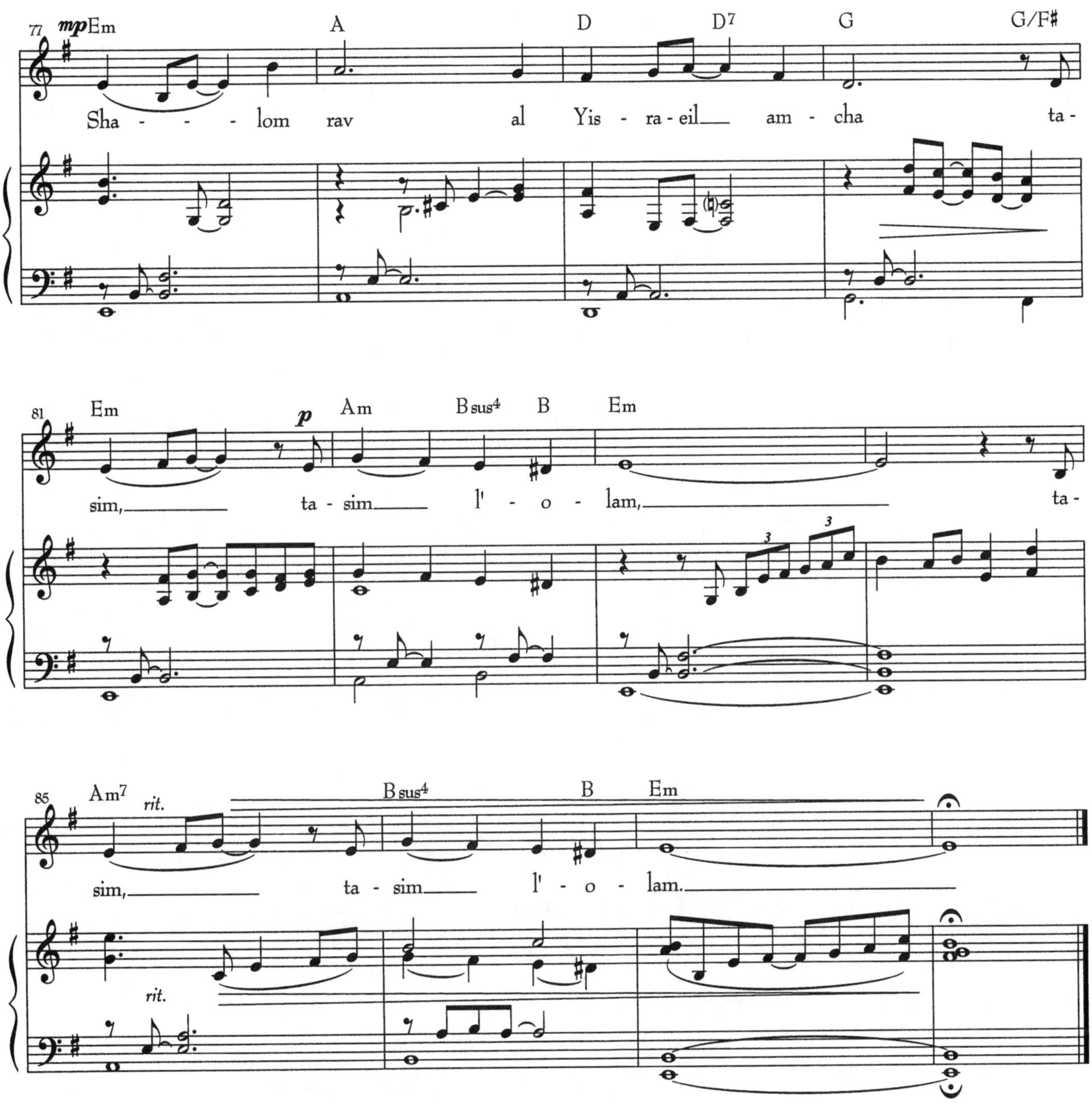

77 mp Em A D D7 G G/F♯
Sha - - - lom rav al Yis - ra - eil am - cha ta -
81 Em p Am Bsus4 B Em
sim, ta - sim l' - o - lam, ta -
85 Am7 rit. Bsus4 B Em
sim, ta - sim l' - o - lam.
rit.

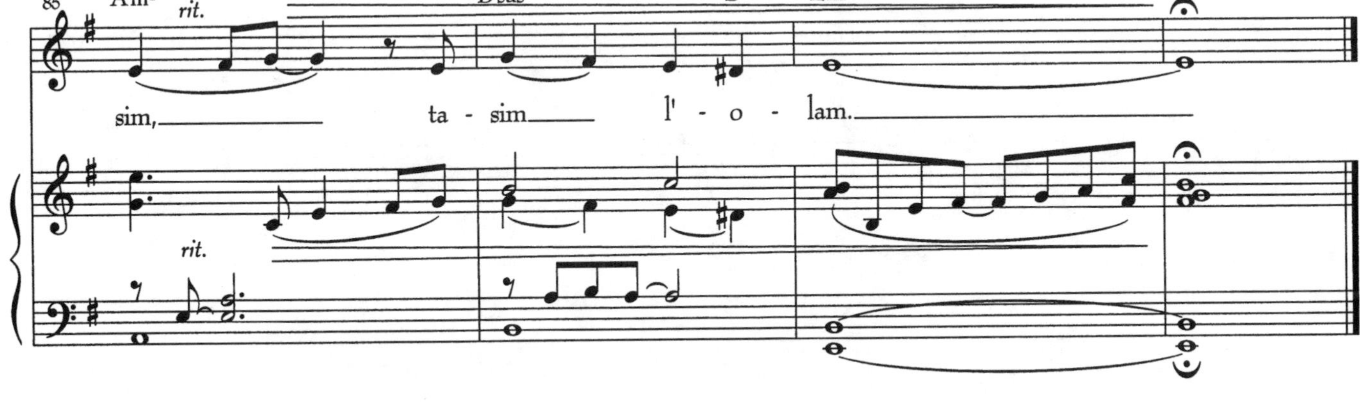

O grant abundant peace to Your people Israel forever. For You are the Sovereign of peace. May it please You to bless us and to bless all Your people Israel with Your peace at all times and at all hours.

שָׁלוֹם רָב עַל־יִשְׂרָאֵל עַמְּךָ תָּשִׂים לְעוֹלָם.
כִּי אַתָּה הוּא מֶלֶךְ אָדוֹן לְכָל הַשָּׁלוֹם.
וְטוֹב בְּעֵינֶיךָ לְבָרֵךְ אֶת־עַמְּךָ יִשְׂרָאֵל
בְּכָל־עֵת וּבְכָל־שָׁעָה בִּשְׁלוֹמֶךָ.

Shalom Rav

שלום רב

Music: David Eddleman
Text: Liturgy

CD track (21)

Originally published for SATB choir, solo voice, and keyboard (992029).

15
G/D A/D D Em/G Emsus4/G Em7/A D
cha ta - sim l' - o - - - - - - - - lam. Ki A -
19
D G D G/D C#°/D Dadd9 D G A7
tah hu Me - lech, hu Me - lech A - - - don, hu Me - lech A -
24
Dmaj7 D6 D Em E7 Asus4 A7 D Dsus4 D
don l' - chol ha - sha - lom. V' - tov b' - ei - ne - cha l' - va -
29
G D/G Em7/B - C# D G A7 Dmaj7 D6 G/D A7
reich et am - - cha, l' - va - reich et am - cha Yis - - - ra - - -

34
D
mf
F
Em/F
Dm/G
Am7
Bm
Am7
D
eil b'-chol eit uv'-chol sha-ah bish-lo-me-cha, b'-
mf
39
F
ad lib.
Em/F
Dm/G
Am7
Bm
Am
A
rit.
chol eit uv'-chol sha-ah bish-lo-me-cha.
colla voce
rit.
44
a little slower
f
D
G/D
D
G/D
A7/D
Ba-ruch A-tah, A-do-
a little slower
f
48
Dsus4
D
Gmaj7
Em7
D7
E7
Bm/E
A9sus4
A
nai, A-do-nai, ha-m'-va-reich et a-mo,

O grant abundant peace to Your people Israel forever. For You are the Sovereign of peace. May it please You to bless us and to bless all Your people Israel with Your peace at all times and at all hours. Praised are You, Eternal God, who blesses our people Israel with peace.

שָׁלוֹם רָב עַל־יִשְׂרָאֵל עַמְּךָ תָּשִׂים לְעוֹלָם,
כִּי אַתָּה הוּא מֶלֶךְ אָדוֹן לְכָל הַשָּׁלוֹם.
וְטוֹב בְּעֵינֶיךָ לְבָרֵךְ אֶת־עַמְּךָ יִשְׂרָאֵל
בְּכָל־עֵת וּבְכָל־שָׁעָה בִּשְׁלוֹמֶךָ.
בָּרוּךְ אַתָּה, יְיָ, הַמְבָרֵךְ אֶת־עַמּוֹ יִשְׂרָאֵל בַּשָּׁלוֹם.

Sim Shalom

שים שלום

Music: Michael Isaacson
Text: Liturgy

CD track (17)

Originally published for SATB choir, solo voice, and keyboard (991020).

F Fsus4 Fadd2 Fsus4 F Fadd2 G/F Fadd2
a tempo
chei - nu, A-vi - - - - nu, ba - r'-chei - nu, A-vi - - - -
a tempo
F F/E F/D F/G C/E Dm7 Gm7 C7sus4
nu, ku - la - nu k'-e - - chad, k'-e - chad b' -
Am Gm7 Dm Gm C7/E C7sus4 C7 C7/B♭
accel. Faster ♩. = 72
mf
A♭ A♭/G Fm7
or, b' - or pa-ne - - cha. Ki v'-or pa-
accel.
B♭m9 B♭m/A♭ E♭/G E♭ E♭/D♭ D♭/E♭ B♭m/A♭ A♭/G Fm A♭/E♭
rall.
ne - cha na-ta - ta la - nu, A - do-nai E - lo - hei - nu To -
simile
rall.

D♭ A♭/C B♭m7 Fm Dm7♭5
rat cha - yim v'-a - ha - vat che - sed u - tz'-da -
F6 Dm B♭/D Am/C Dm7
kah u - v'-ra-chah v'-ra-cha - mim v'-cha - yim v'-sha -
sub. mp
Csus4 Tempo I F Fsus4 Fadd2 Fsus4 F
rall.
lom. V' - tov b' - ei-ne - - - - - cha l' - va-
Tempo I
simile
Fadd2 G/F Fadd2 F F/E F/D F/G C/E Dm7
reich et am-cha Yis - ra - eil b'-chol eit uv'-chol sha-

Standard Ending

34 Gm7 C7sus4 | Am Gm7 Dm Gm | C7/E C7sus4

ah bish-lo-me - cha. Ba-ruch A-tah, A-do-nai, ham'-va - reich et a-

simile *rall.*

37 F Fsus4 Csus4 | Fadd2 Fsus4 Fadd2

mo Yis-ra-eil ba-sha-lom, ba-sha-lom.

colla voce *rit.*

High Holy Day Ending

34 Gm7 C7sus4 | Am Gm7 Dm Gm | C7/E Am

rit. *mp*

ah bish-lo-me - cha b'-sei-fer cha-yim b'-ra - chah b'-sei-fer cha-yim, b'-

simile *rit.*

37 Dm Dm/C | B♭maj7 Dm/A Gm Dm | Gm Gm/F C/E C7

sei - fer cha-yim b'-ra-chah v'-sha - lom u-far-na-sah to - - - -

Grant peace, happiness, blessing, kindness and mercy to us and to all Israel, Your people. Bless us, our Creator, one and all, with the light of Your presence; for by that light You have given us the law of life: to love kindness, justice, and mercy, to seek blessing, life, and peace. May it please You to bless us and all Your people Israel with peace at all times.

Standard Ending: *Praised are You, Eternal God, who blesses our people Israel with peace.*

High Holy Day Ending: *Blessing, peace, and sustenance in the Book of Life. May we and all Your people Israel be remembered and written by You for a good life and for peace. Praised are You, Eternal God, the Source of peace.*

שִׂים שָׁלוֹם, טוֹבָה וּבְרָכָה חֵן וָחֶסֶד וְרַחֲמִים, עָלֵינוּ
וְעַל־כָּל־יִשְׂרָאֵל עַמֶּךָ. בָּרְכֵנוּ, אָבִינוּ, כֻּלָּנוּ כְּאֶחָד,
בְּאוֹר פָּנֶיךָ, כִּי בְאוֹר פָּנֶיךָ נָתַתָּ לָּנוּ, יְיָ אֱלֹהֵינוּ,
תּוֹרַת חַיִּים וְאַהֲבַת חֶסֶד, וּצְדָקָה וּבְרָכָה
וְרַחֲמִים וְחַיִּים וְשָׁלוֹם. וְטוֹב בְּעֵינֶיךָ לְבָרֵךְ
אֶת־עַמְּךָ יִשְׂרָאֵל בְּכָל־עֵת וּבְכָל־שָׁעָה בִּשְׁלוֹמֶךָ.

Standard Ending:

בָּרוּךְ אַתָּה, יְיָ, הַמְבָרֵךְ אֶת־עַמּוֹ יִשְׂרָאֵל בַּשָּׁלוֹם.

High Holy Day Ending:

בְּסֵפֶר חַיִּים בְּרָכָה וְשָׁלוֹם וּפַרְנָסָה טוֹבָה. נִזָּכֵר
וְנִכָּתֵב לְפָנֶיךָ אֲנַחְנוּ וְכָל עַמְּךָ יִשְׂרָאֵל לְחַיִּים
טוֹבִים וּלְשָׁלוֹם. בָּרוּךְ אַתָּה, יְיָ, עוֹשֵׂה הַשָּׁלוֹם.

Elohai N'tzor

אלהי נצר

Music: Danny Maseng, arr. J. Mark Dunn
Text: Sabbath liturgy

CD track (19)

7
G
D7sus4
G
D7sus4
B
Cadd9
D7sus4/G
G
hai,
E-lo-hai.
P'tach,
p'tach li-bi.
hai,
E-lo-hai.
P'tach,
p'tach li-bi.
hai,
E-lo-hai.
P'tach,
p'tach li-bi.
7
12
G
D7sus4
Cadd9
Em6
P'tach,
p'tach li-bi
p'tach li-
P'tach,
p'tach li-bi
p'tach li-
P'tach,
p'tach li-bi
p'tach li-
12

17
Am7
D7sus4
D7
C
G
D7sus4
bi b'-to-ra-te-cha. N'-tzor l'-sho-ni mei-ra. us'-fa-
bi b'-to-ra-te-cha. N'-tzor l'-sho-ni mei-ra. us'-fa-
bi b'-to-ra-te-cha. N'-tzor l'-sho-ni mei-ra. us'-fa-
17
21
G
D7sus4
G
D7sus4
G
D7sus4
tai mi-da-beir mir-mah, v'-lim-ka-l'-lai naf-shi-ti-dom, v'-naf-shi ke-a-far la-kol ti-h'-yeh. E-lo-
tai mi-da-beir mir-mah, v'-lim-ka-l'-lai naf-shi-ti-dom, v'-naf-shi ke-a-far la-kol ti-h'-yeh. E-lo-
tai mi-da-beir mir-mah, v'-lim-ka-l'-lai naf-shi-ti-dom, v'-naf-shi ke-a-far la-kol ti-h'-yeh. E-lo-
21

G D7sus4 G D7sus4 G D7sus4 G D7sus4
hai, E-lo - hai. E-lo - hai, n'-tzor l'-sho-ni mei-ra. us'-fa-
hai, E-lo - hai. E-lo - hai, n'-tzor l'-sho-ni mei-ra. us'-fa-
hai, E-lo - hai. E-lo - hai, n'-tzor l'-sho-ni mei-ra. us'-fa-
G D7sus4 G D7sus4 G D7sus4
tai mi-da-beir mir-mah, v'-lim-ka-l'-lai naf-shi-ti-dom, v'-naf-shi ke-a-far la-kol ti-h'-yeh. E-lo-
tai mi-da-beir mir-mah, v'-lim-ka-l'-lai naf-shi-ti-dom, v'-naf-shi ke-a-far la-kol ti-h'-yeh. E-lo-
tai mi-da-beir mir-mah, v'-lim-ka-l'-lai naf-shi-ti-dom, v'-naf-shi ke-a-far la-kol ti-h'-yeh. E-lo-

O God, keep my tongue from evil and my lips from deceit. Help me to be silent in the face of derision, humble in the presence of all. Open my heart to Your Torah. May the words of my mouth and the meditations of my heart be acceptable to You, Eternal One, my Rock and my Redeemer.

אֱלֹהַי, נְצֹר לְשׁוֹנִי מֵרָע וּשְׂפָתַי מִדַּבֵּר מִרְמָה, וְלִמְקַלְלַי נַפְשִׁי תִדּוֹם, וְנַפְשִׁי כֶּעָפָר לַכֹּל תִּהְיֶה. פְּתַח לִבִּי בְּתוֹרָתֶךָ. יִהְיוּ לְרָצוֹן אִמְרֵי־פִי וְהֶגְיוֹן לִבִּי לְפָנֶיךָ, יְיָ, צוּרִי וְגוֹאֲלִי.

Yih'yu L'ratzon/Oseh Shalom יהיו לרצון\עושה שלום

Music: *Bonia Shur*
Text: *Liturgy*

CD track (14)

May the words of my mouth and the meditations of my heart be acceptable to You, Eternal One, my Rock and my Redeemer.

יִהְיוּ לְרָצוֹן אִמְרֵי־פִי וְהֶגְיוֹן לִבִּי
לְפָנֶיךָ, יְיָ, צוּרִי וְגוֹאֲלִי.

Oseh Shalom

עושה שלום

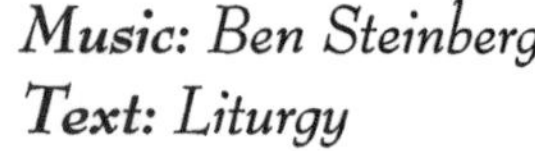

Music: Ben Steinberg
Text: Liturgy

CD track (18)

(gtr. capo 3)

O - seh sha - lom bi-m'-ro - mav Hu

4 ya - a - seh sha - lom a - lei - nu v' - al kol Yis - - - ra -

7 eil, v' - al kol, v' - al kol Yis - ra -

(Organ)

Originally published in *Kol Shalom: Voice of Peace* for Cantor, SATB choir, organ, and optional strings (992031), and for treble choir and organ (991553).

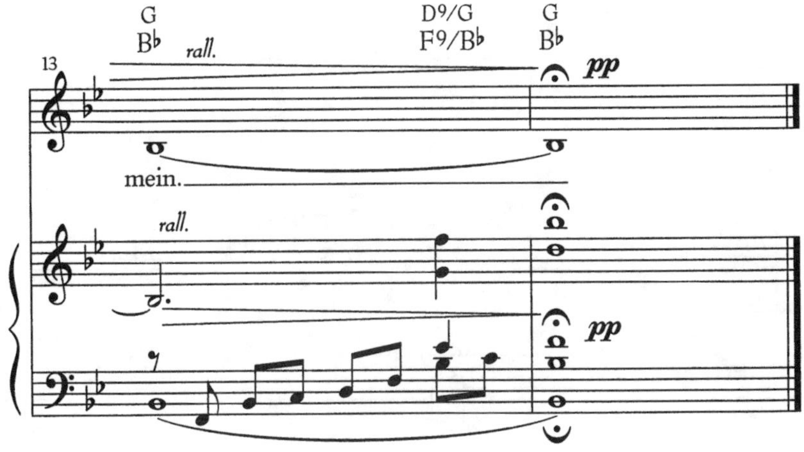

May the One who causes peace to reign in the high heavens let peace descend on us and on all Israel, and let us say: Amen.

עֹשֶׂה שָׁלוֹם בִּמְרוֹמָיו, הוּא יַעֲשֶׂה שָׁלוֹם עָלֵינוּ וְעַל כָּל־יִשְׂרָאֵל, וְאִמְרוּ: אָמֵן.

Lo Yisa Goi

לא ישא גוי

Music & English text: Eric Komar & Jordan Franzel
Hebrew text: Isaiah 2:4

CD track (7)

C/G Am7 Bm7 Em7
tion, a ves-sel of light that shined with
Am7 C/D D G
kind - ness and love. Then ev-ery-thing scat - tered in ev - ery di-rec -
C/G Bm7 Em7
tion. What now is be-low once was u -
Am7 D D#o Em
nit - ed a - bove. Cain killed A - bel in a jeal-ous rage;

Cmaj7
Fmaj7
now ev - ery na - tion has a war to wage.
We watch the blood - shed help -
mf
D
Bm7
Cadd9
mp
Am7
less - ly with no words to say.
Why can't we live with - out
C/D
D
Ch
G
mp (Last time: f)
Em7
Em11
Bm
C
hate to - day?
Lo yi - sa goi el goi che - rev,
Am7
G/B
Cmaj7
D#o
Em7
lo yil - m' - du od mil - cha - mah.
Lo yi - sa

Cmaj9 G/D D/C G/B G♭7♭9/B♭ Am7 Bm7 Cmaj9
53
mf
goi el goi che - - - rev, lo yil - m'- du od
Dsus4 C/D to Coda 1. G (2nd ending: m. 88) C/G D
57
mil - - - cha - - - mah.
to Coda
mp
sub. f
V2 G C/G
62
mp
I dream of a time of more un-der-stand - ing.
Bm7 Em7 Am7 D
66
I hope for a day when peo - ple of all lands join as one.

70
G
mf
C/G
I pray for a New Age with - out fear; we would all
mf
73
Bm7
Em7
Am7
3
live from year to year, neigh-bor and neigh - - - bor, in the World Yet to
3
77
D
D#°
Em
f
Cmaj7
Come. With guns in streets and bombs in stores, eth-nic cleans - ing and ho-
f
81
Fmaj7
ly wars, what les-sons have our chil - dren learned from a

D Bm7 Cadd9 Am7 Dsus4 D
mf
world this way, when they shall lead us to peace we pray.
2. G G7 Accelerando ♩= 120 Br C Bm7
f
mah.
Where is the land flow - ing with
Em7 E♭maj7 Cm7 Am7♭5
milk and hon - ey, when all we see is a world filled with
D Cmaj7 Bm7
ff
blood and tears? If we can de - stroy then we can re - pair,

101
Em
A/C♯
Am/C
Am7
making plowshares from swords and pruning hooks from
105
Dsus4
D
D.S. al Coda
spears.
106
Em
Em/D♯
Em7/D
mah,
108
A9/C♯
rit.
mp
Am7
Bm7
Cmaj9
Dsus4
D7
lo yil - m'-du od mil - cha -
112
G
C/G
G
mah.
molto rit.
p

Al Sh'loshah D'varim

על שלשה דברים

Music: Steve Dropkin, arr. J. Mark Dunn
Text: Pirkei Avot 1:2

CD track 25

D A E

A D A E D A

3

Al sh'lo-shah d'-va - rim, al sh'lo - shah d'-va -

6

E A D A to Coda E

rim ha - o - lam o-meid.__ Al sh'lo - shah d'-va - rim ha - o -

to Coda

9
D
E
1. A
2. A
lam, ha - o - lam o - - - - meid:
meid.
B
12
F♯m
E
D
E
A
F♯m
E
Al ha - To - rah v' - al ha - a - vo - dah v' - al g' - mi - lut cha - sa -
15
F♯m
D
E
A
F♯m
dim.
Al ha - To - rah v' - al ha - a - vo - dah v' -
18
D
G
E
D.S. al Coda
al g' - mi - lut cha - sa - dim.
D.S. al Coda

The world stands on three things: on Torah, on worship, and on acts of loving kindness.

עַל-שְׁלֹשָׁה דְבָרִים הָעוֹלָם עוֹמֵד:
עַל הַתּוֹרָה וְעַל הָעֲבוֹדָה וְעַל גְּמִילוּת חֲסָדִים.

Al Sh'loshah D'varim

על שלושה דברים

Music: Ben Steinberg
Text: Pirkei Avot 1:2

CD track (12)

Orignally published in *Avodat HaKodesh Sacred Service for Sabbath Worship* for SATB choir, solo voice, and organ, with optional woodwind quartet (991350).

The world stands on three things: on Torah, on worship, and on acts of loving kindness.

עַל-שְׁלשָׁה דְבָרִים הָעוֹלָם עוֹמֵד:
עַל הַתּוֹרָה וְעַל הָעֲבוֹדָה וְעַל גְּמִילוּת חֲסָדִים.

Adon Olam

אדון עולם

Music: traditional, arr. Bonia Shur
Text: Liturgy

CD track 24

Am Am7/C D/A E Am6 Am/C
Cm Cm7/E♭ F/C G Cm6 Cm/E♭
11
a - - - cha - rei kich - lot ha - kol, l' - va - - - - do yim -
Hu E - chad v' - ein shei - ni, l' - ham - - - shil lo l' -
Am7 Dm/F E Dm7 Dm7/F G C
Cm7 Fm/A♭ G Fm7 Fm7/A♭ B♭ E♭
14
loch no - ra. V' - Hu ha - yah, v' - Hu ho - veh, v' -
hach - bi - rah. B' - li rei - shit, b' - li tach - lit v' -
Am7 Dm/F Am7/C E
Cm7 Fm/A♭ Cm7/E♭ G
1. Am E Am
Cm G Cm
2. Am E Am
Cm G Cm
17
Hu yih - yeh b' - tif - a - rah. V' - ha - mis - rah.
lo ha - oz v' -

Cm G Am Dm7 Am Em/G
E♭m B♭ Cm Fm7 Cm Gm/B♭
20
p leggiero
La la la la la la la. La la la la la la la. La la la la la la la.
p leggiero
Dm7/F E Am Em/G C Dm7/F
Fm7/A♭ G Cm Gm/B♭ E♭ Fm7/A♭
23
mf
La la la la la. La la la la la la la. La la la la la la la.
mf
Am Em/G F Dm7 Am Am Am/C
Cm Gm/B♭ A♭ Fm7 Cm Cm (Cm/E♭)
26
S/A:
Alto:
mf
La la la la la la la. La la la la la. V' - Hu Ei - li v' -
ya - - - - do af -
T/B:
Tenor:
mf
La la la la la la la. La la la la la.
V' - Hu Ei - li v' -
B' - ya - do af -

Am7 F E Am Am/C Am F E Dm7 Dm7/F
Cm7 A♭ G Cm Cm/E♭ Cm A♭ G Fm7 Fm7/A♭
28
A
chai go - a - li v' - tzur___ chev - li b' - eit tza - rah. V' - Hu ni - si u -
kid ru - chi b' - eit___ i - shan v' - a - i - rah. V' - im ru - chi g' -
T
chai___ go - a - li v' - tzur___ chev - li b'-eit tza-rah. V'-Hu ni - si___ u -
kid___ ru - chi b' - eit___ i - shan v'-a - i - rah. V'-im ru - chi___ g' -
mf
G C Am Dm/F Am/C E Am E Am
B♭ E♭ Cm Fm/A♭ Cm/E♭ G Cm G Cm
32
A
ma - nos___ li, m' - nat ko - si___ b' - yom ek - ra.
vi - ya - ti. A - do - nai li___ v' - lo i - ra.
T
ma - nos___ li, m' - nat ko - si b' - yom b' - yom ek - ra.
vi - ya - ti. A - do - nai li v' - lo v' - lo i - ra.

35
Cm Eb♭m G B♭ Am Cm Dm7 Fm7 Am7 Cm7 Em/G Gm/B♭ Dm7/F Fm7/A♭ E G
S
mf leggiero
La la la la. La la la la la la. La la la la la la.
A
mf leggiero
La la la la la la la. La la la la la la la. La la la la la la la. La la la la la.
T/B
mf leggiero
La la la la la la la. La la la la la la la. La la la la la la la. La la la la la.
mf leggiero
39
Am Cm Em/G Gm/B♭ C E♭ Dm7/F Fm7/A♭ Am Cm Em/G Gm/B♭ 1. F A♭ Dm7 Fm7 Am Cm
S
f
La la la la la la la. La la la la la la la. La la la la la la la. La la la la la.
A
f
mf
La la la la la la la. La la la la la la la. La la la la la la la. La la la la la. B'-
T/B
f
La la la la la la la. La la la la la la la. La la la la la la la. La la la la la.
1.
f

You are our Eternal God, who reigned before any being had yet been created; when all was done according to Your will, already You were Ruler.

אֲדוֹן עוֹלָם, אֲשֶׁר מָלַךְ, בְּטֶרֶם כָּל־יְצִיר נִבְרָא,
לְעֵת נַעֲשָׂה בְחֶפְצוֹ כֹּל, אֲזַי מֶלֶךְ שְׁמוֹ נִקְרָא.

And after all ceases to be, still You will rule in solitary majesty; You were, are, and will be in glory.

וְאַחֲרֵי כִּכְלוֹת הַכֹּל, לְבַדּוֹ יִמְלוֹךְ נוֹרָא,
וְהוּא הָיָה, וְהוּא הֹוֶה, וְהוּא יִהְיֶה בְּתִפְאָרָה.

And You are One; none other can compare to or consort with the Eternal. You are without beginning, without end. To You belong power and dominion.

וְהוּא אֶחָד, וְאֵין שֵׁנִי, לְהַמְשִׁיל לוֹ, לְהַחְבִּירָה,
בְּלִי רֵאשִׁית, בְּלִי תַכְלִית, וְלוֹ הָעֹז וְהַמִּשְׂרָה.

And You are my God, my living Redeemer, my Rock in times of trouble and distress. You are my banner and my refuge, my benefactor when I call on You.

וְהוּא אֵלִי, וְחַי גֹּאֲלִי, וְצוּר חֶבְלִי בְּעֵת צָרָה,
וְהוּא נִסִּי וּמָנוֹס לִי, מְנָת כּוֹסִי בְּיוֹם אֶקְרָא.

Into Your hands I entrust my spirit, when I sleep and when I wake, and with my spirit my body also; the Eternal is with me, I will not fear.

בְּיָדוֹ אַפְקִיד רוּחִי בְּעֵת אִישַׁן וְאָעִירָה,
וְעִם־רוּחִי גְּוִיָּתִי: יְיָ לִי, וְלֹא אִירָא.

Adon Olam

אדון עולם

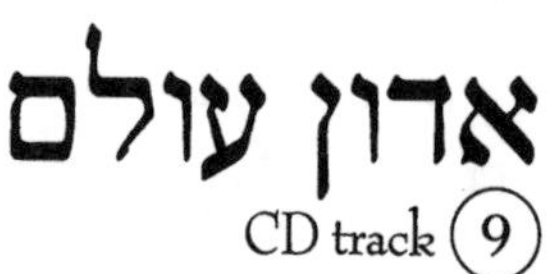

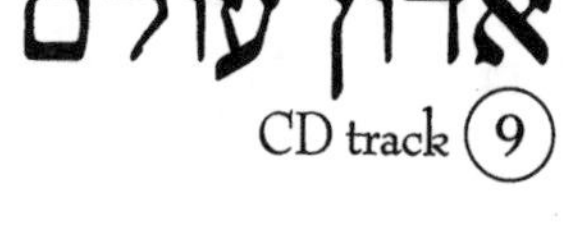

Music: Melody from the Isle of Djerba, arr. Ben Steinberg
Text: Liturgy

CD track 9

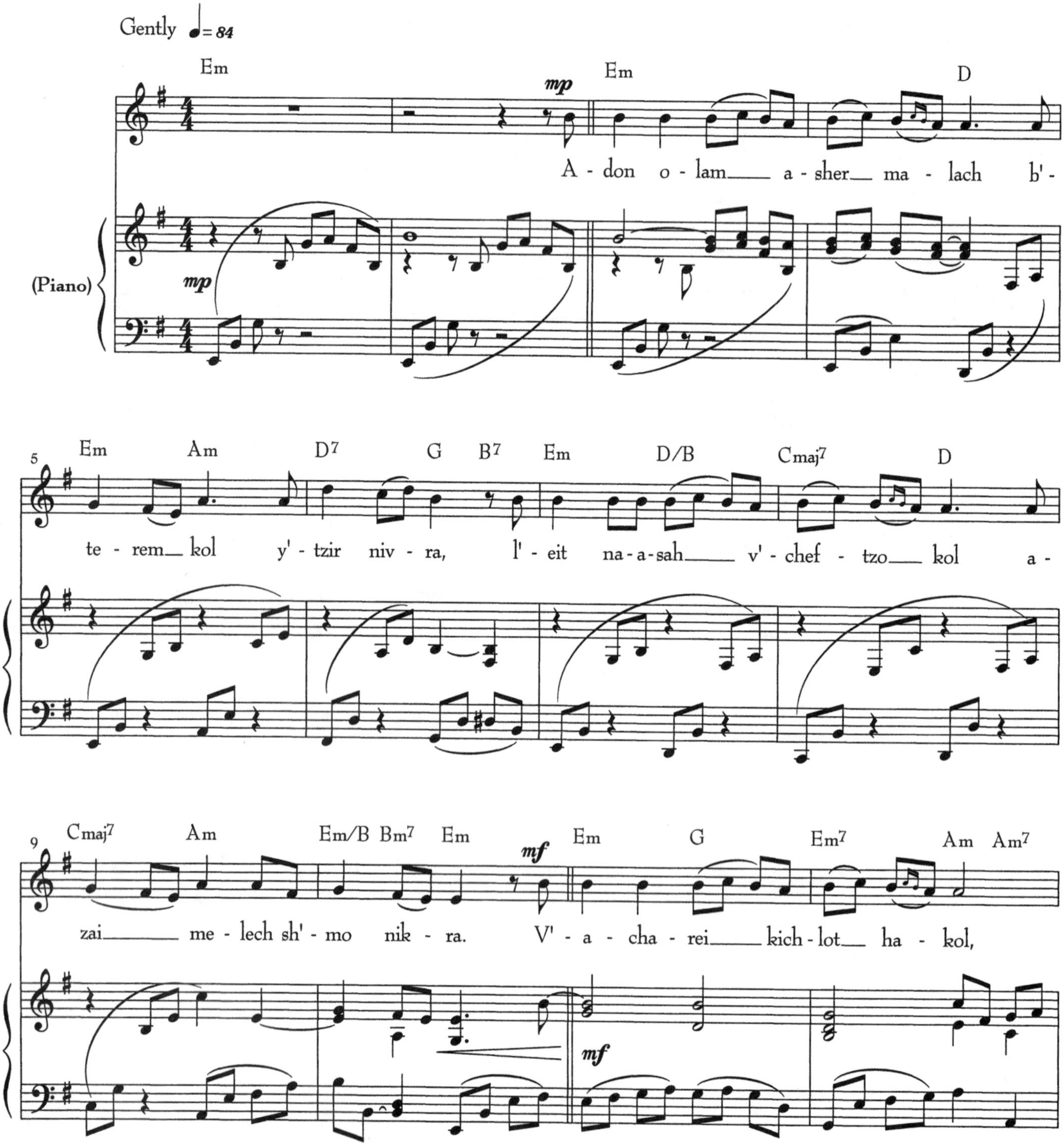
Gently ♩= 84
Em
mp
Em
D
A - don o - lam a - sher ma - lach b'-
(Piano)
5
Em Am D7 G B7 Em D/B Cmaj7 D
te - rem kol y' - tzir niv - ra, l' - eit na - a - sah v' - chef - tzo kol a -
9
Cmaj7 Am Em/B Bm7 Em Em G Em7 Am Am7
mf
zai me - lech sh' - mo nik - ra. V' - a - cha - rei kich - lot ha - kol,

Originally published for 2 voices, piano, and flute (991227).

Em Am D/F♯ G Am7 Bm Em Bm Em D D7
l' - va - do yim - loch no - ra, v' - Hu ha - ya, v' - Hu ho - veh, v' -
Cmaj7 Am D/F♯ G/B Bm7 Em Bm Em Bm Am/C Bm7
Hu yih' - yeh b' - tif - a - rah. V' -
mp
Em Bm7sus4 Em D G Am D C/D G D
Hu E - chad v' - ein shei - ni l' - ham - shil lo, l' - hach - bi - rah, b' -
mp
Em G Em7 Am Em Am Em7 Bm Em
li rei - shit b' - li tach - lit, v' - lo ha - oz v' - ha - mis - rah. V' -
mf

29
G Am Am7 Em Am D/F♯ G Am7 Bm
Hu Ei - li, v' - chai go - a - li, v' - tzur chev - li b' - eit tza - rah, v'-
mf
33
Em Bm Em D D7 Cmaj7 Am Em/B Em7 Em
Hu ni - si u - ma - nos li, m' - nat ko - si b' - yom ek - ra.
37
Em Bm Am Bm7 Em Bm7sus4 Em D
f
B' - ya - do af - kid - ru - chi b'-
41
G Am D C/D G D Em G Em7 Am
eit i - shan v' - a - i - rah, v' - im ru - chi g' - vi - ya - ti: A - do-

אֲדוֹן עוֹלָם, אֲשֶׁר מָלַךְ, בְּטֶרֶם כָּל־יְצִיר נִבְרָא,
לְעֵת נַעֲשָׂה בְחֶפְצוֹ כֹּל, אֲזַי מֶלֶךְ שְׁמוֹ נִקְרָא.

You are our Eternal God, who reigned before any being had yet been created; when all was done according to Your will, already You were Ruler.

וְאַחֲרֵי כִּכְלוֹת הַכֹּל, לְבַדּוֹ יִמְלוֹךְ נוֹרָא,
וְהוּא הָיָה, וְהוּא הֹוֶה, וְהוּא יִהְיֶה בְּתִפְאָרָה.

And after all ceases to be, still You will rule in solitary majesty; You were, are, and will be in glory.

וְהוּא אֶחָד, וְאֵין שֵׁנִי, לְהַמְשִׁיל לוֹ, לְהַחְבִּירָה,
בְּלִי רֵאשִׁית, בְּלִי תַכְלִית, וְלוֹ הָעֹז וְהַמִּשְׂרָה.

And You are One; none other can compare to or consort with the Eternal. You are without beginning, without end. To You belong power and dominion.

וְהוּא אֵלִי, וְחַי גּוֹאֲלִי, וְצוּר חֶבְלִי בְּעֵת צָרָה,
וְהוּא נִסִּי וּמָנוֹס לִי, מְנָת כּוֹסִי בְּיוֹם אֶקְרָא.

And You are my God, my living Redeemer, my Rock in times of trouble and distress. You are my banner and my refuge, my benefactor when I call on You.

בְּיָדוֹ אַפְקִיד רוּחִי בְּעֵת אִישַׁן וְאָעִירָה,
וְעִם־רוּחִי גְּוִיָּתִי: יְיָ לִי, וְלֹא אִירָא.

Into Your hands I entrust my spirit, when I sleep and when I wake, and with my spirit my body also; the Eternal is with me, I will not fear.

Adon Olam

אדון עולם

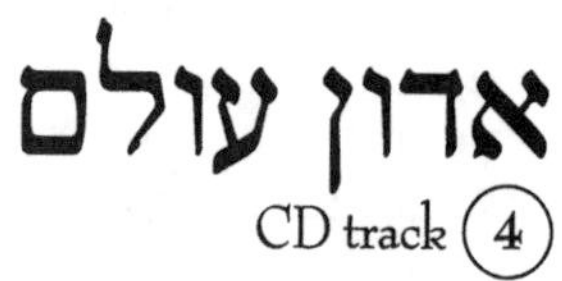

Music: Aminadav Aloni, arr. Christopher Hardin
Text: Liturgy

CD track 4

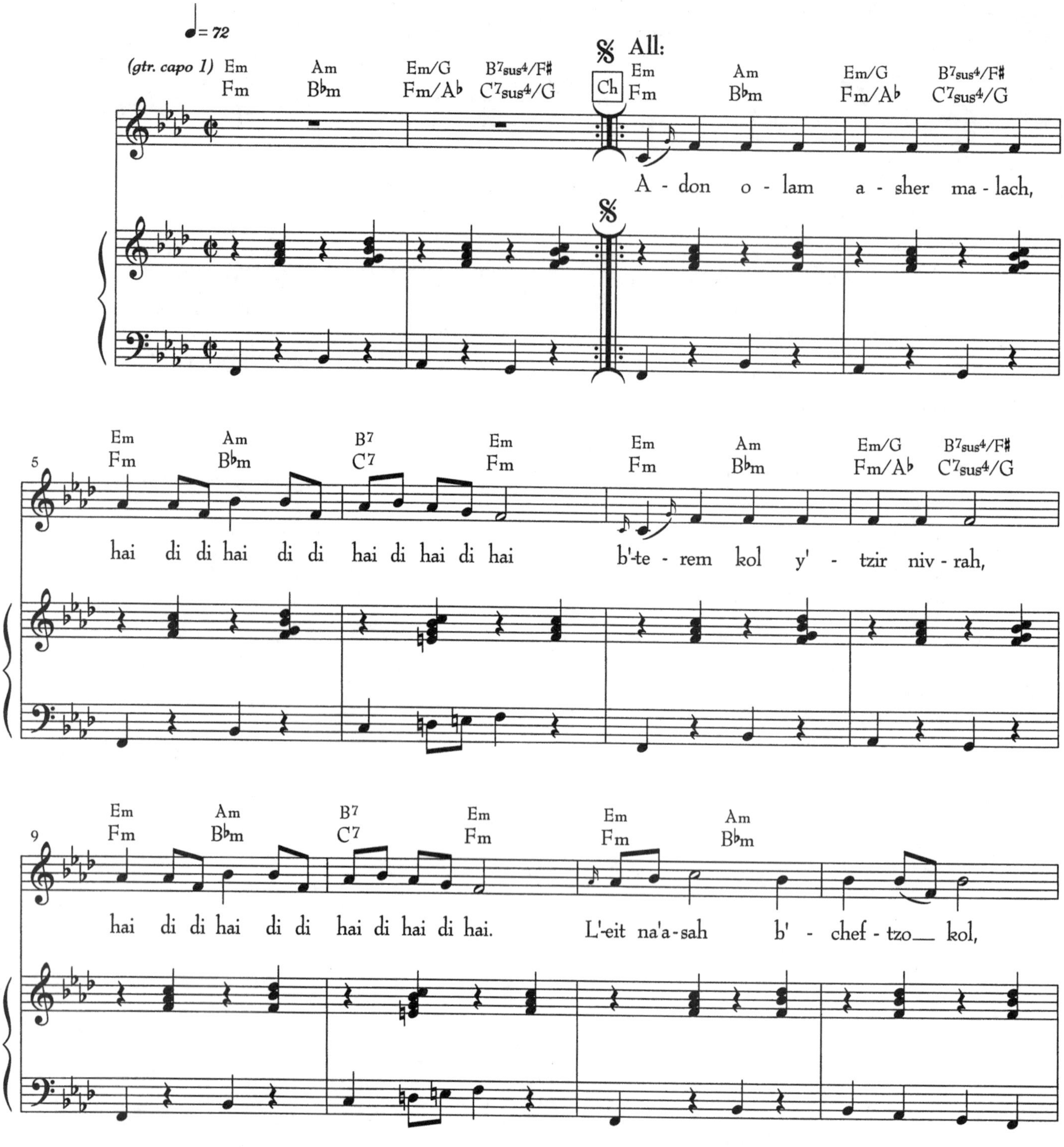
♩= 72
(gtr. capo 1)
All:
Ch
Em Am Em/G B7sus4/F♯
Fm B♭m Fm/A♭ C7sus4/G
A - don o - lam a - sher ma - lach,
5
Em Am B7 Em
Fm B♭m C7 Fm
hai di di hai di di hai di hai di hai
b'-te - rem kol y' - tzir niv - rah,
9
hai di di hai di di hai di hai di hai.
L'-eit na'a-sah b' - chef - tzo kol,

Originally published in *Shir Chadash: A Friday Night Evening Service for Cantor, Children's Choir, and Teenage or Adult Choir.* Commissioned by Cantor Nathan Lam and Midway Jewish Center, Syosset, NY. (993151).

D7
E♭7
G
A♭
B7
C7
Em
Fm
Am
B♭m
Last time: to Coda
hai dai dai di dai di hai di hai, a-zai me - lech sh'mo nik - ra,
Last time: to Coda
Em/B
Fm/C
B7
C7
1., 2.
Em
Fm
Solo:
V1&2
hai dai hai dai dai.
1. V' - a - cha-rei kich-lot ha-kol l' -
2. V' - Hu E-chad v' - ein shei-ni, l' -
F♯7
G7
va - do yim - loch no - ra, v' - Hu ha-yah v' -
ham - shil lo l' - hach - bi - rah, b' - li rei-shit b' -
B
C
All:
Hu ho-veh v' - Hu yih-yeh b'-tif - a - rah,
li tach-lit, v' - lo ha-oz v'-ha - mis - rah,
Hai di dai di dai di

3., 4. Solo: V3&4

Em Fm | Em Fm | Am B♭m | B7 C7 | Em Fm

27 dai. 3. V' - Hu Ei - li v' - chai go - a - li, v' - tzur chev - li b' -
4. B' - ya - do af - kid ru - chi, b' - eit i - shan v' -

F♯7 G7 | B7 C7 | Em Fm | Am B♭m | F♯7 G7

31 eit tza - rah, V' - Hu ni - si u - ma - nos li, m' - nat ko - si b' - yom ek -
a - i - rah, v' - im ru - chi g' - vi - ya - ti, A - do - nai li v' - lo i -

B C | All: D.S. al Coda

35 ra, ra, } Hai di dai di dai di

D.S. al Coda

Em/B Fm/C | B7 C7 | Em Fm

36 hai dai hai dai dai

You are our Eternal God, who reigned before any being had yet been created; when all was done according to Your will, already You were Ruler.

אֲדוֹן עוֹלָם, אֲשֶׁר מָלַךְ, בְּטֶרֶם כָּל־יְצִיר נִבְרָא,
לְעֵת נַעֲשָׂה בְחֶפְצוֹ כֹּל, אֲזַי מֶלֶךְ שְׁמוֹ נִקְרָא.

And after all ceases to be, still You will rule in solitary majesty; You were, are, and will be in glory.

וְאַחֲרֵי כִּכְלוֹת הַכֹּל, לְבַדּוֹ יִמְלוֹךְ נוֹרָא,
וְהוּא הָיָה, וְהוּא הֹוֶה, וְהוּא יִהְיֶה בְּתִפְאָרָה.

And You are One; none other can compare to or consort with the Eternal. You are without beginning, without end. To You belong power and dominion.

וְהוּא אֶחָד, וְאֵין שֵׁנִי, לְהַמְשִׁיל לוֹ, לְהַחְבִּירָה,
בְּלִי רֵאשִׁית, בְּלִי תַכְלִית, וְלֹא הָעֹז וְהַמִּשְׂרָה.

And You are my God, my living Redeemer, my Rock in times of trouble and distress. You are my banner and my refuge, my benefactor when I call on You.

וְהוּא אֵלִי, וְחַי גּוֹאֲלִי, וְצוּר חֶבְלִי בְּעֵת צָרָה,
וְהוּא נִסִּי וּמָנוֹס לִי, מְנָת כּוֹסִי בְּיוֹם אֶקְרָא.

Into Your hands I entrust my spirit, when I sleep and when I wake, and with my spirit my body also; the Eternal is with me, I will not fear.

בְּיָדוֹ אַפְקִיד רוּחִי בְּעֵת אִישַׁן וְאָעִירָה,
וְעִם־רוּחִי גְּוִיָּתִי: יְיָ לִי, וְלֹא אִירָא.

Adonai Li

יי לי

CD track (20)

Music: Bruce Benson & Don Rossoff
arr. Andrea Jill Higgins, ed. J. Mark Dunn
Text: Liturgy, from Adon Olam

Originally published for SAB choir, piano, and flute (993214).

9
Am G/B C F G C
nai li, v' - lo i - - - ra. A - do -
13
Am Em Dm7 Gsus4 G
nai li, v' - lo i - - - - ra. A - do -
mf
17
Am G/B C C/E F G C C7
f
mp
nai li, v' - lo i - - - ra.
poco

B
21
F
mf
Em
cresc.
Dm
D7/A
Gsus4
G
B'-ya-do af-kid ru-chi b'-eit i-shan v'-a-i-rah, v'-
mf
25
F
E7
Am
Dm7/F
Dm7
f
Gsus4
G
im ru----chi g'-vi---ya----ti. A-do-
f
C
29
Am
G/B
C
F
G
C
mf
nai li, v'-lo i----ra. A-do-
f
mf

33
Am G/B C F G C
mp
nai li, v'-lo i - - - ra. A-do-
mp
37
Am Em Fadd9 B♭ Gsus4 G
mf
nai li, v'-lo i - - - ra. A-do-
41
Am G/B C C/E F G Cmaj7/E
mp
nai li, v'-lo i - - - ra. Hm.
mf
mp

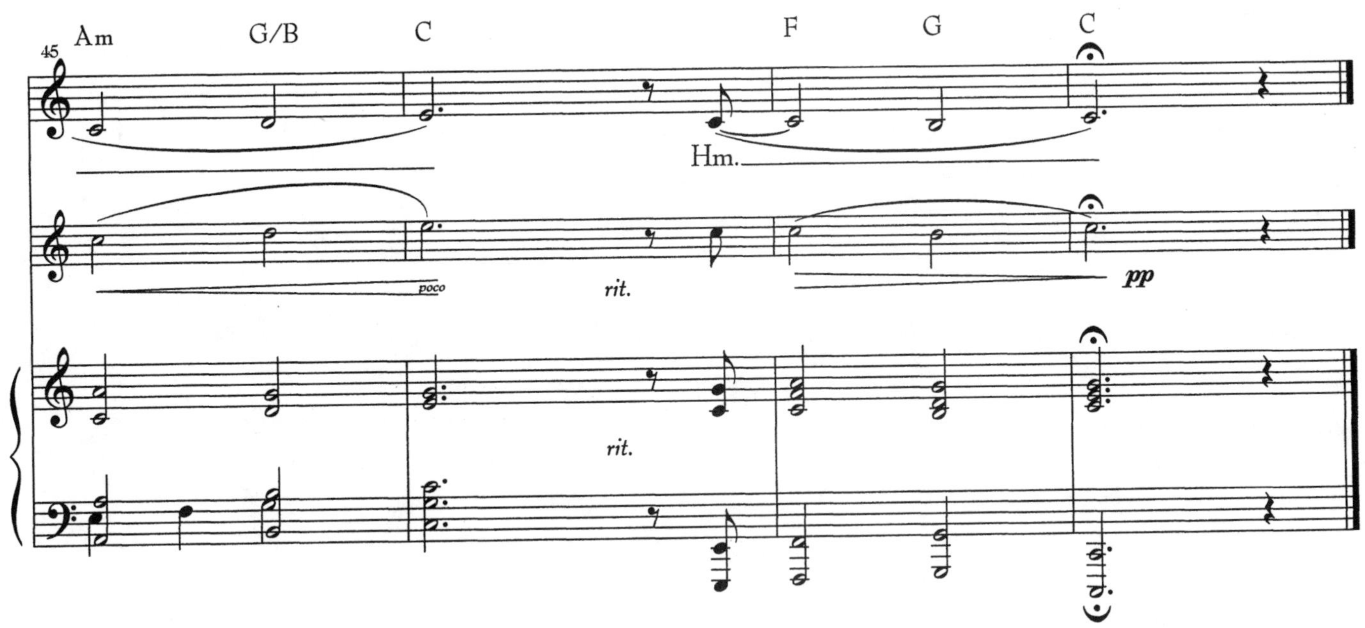

The Eternal is with me, I will not fear.
Into Your hands I entrust my spirit, when I sleep and when I wake, and with my spirit my body also;
the Eternal is with me, I will not fear.

יְיָ לִי, וְלֹא אִירָא.
בְּיָדוֹ אַפְקִיד רוּחִי בְּעֵת אִישַׁן וְאָעִירָה,
וְעִם־רוּחִי גְּוִיָּתִי: יְיָ לִי, וְלֹא אִירָא.

Niggunim
(wordless melodies)

Niggun

CD track (16)

Niggun "Lubavitcher"

CD track (3)

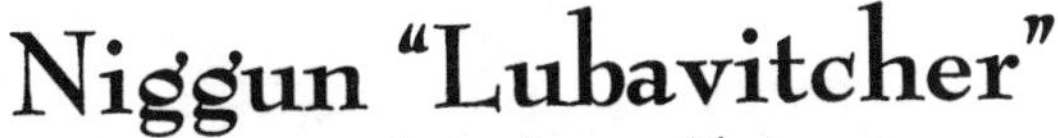
(For the late Lubavitcher Rebbe)
Arr. Jeff Klepper

Niggun "Bialik"

CD track 23

Also published for SATB choir, arr. Binder. (990724).

Niggun "Y'did Nefesh"

CD track (11)

Niggun

Music: attrib. to B. Kazansky

CD track (26)

Niggun "Kvell"

Music: Joel N. Eglash

CD track (28)